"How To Make Thousands Of Dollars Every Month… Doing Just One Thing!"

I0479933

Dr. Ivan Carney

SCAN ME

DEDICATION

This book is dedicated to all my authors, people that have invested in me, my parents who made me who I am, Celia Garcia, Joel Bauer, my mentor, Duane Carney, Dan Gallapoo, Marlon Sanders, my son Christopher Carney, his family, and my grandchildren. I'm leaving a lot of people out, but I want you to know, if you know who I am, I love you and care about your success. That is a truthful statement and it comes from my heart. Be safe.

CONTENTS

ACKNOWLEDGMENTS

I had to look at other books to make sure I constructed a good acknowledgments page, but you know what, I want to acknowledge you. You're reading this book and to me, that is who I want to acknowledge.

CHAPTER 1

WHY YOU HAVE TO HAVE A SHORT
LEAD MAGNET BOOK

JIM, a business consultant, understood the power of using his book as his ultimate business card. He was 57 years old, but he was the type of man that was growing and learning, every single day.

He'd go to bed at night and have stacks of books on his nightstand.

Why?

He might read three or four pages from a couple of books or maybe just a recent newsletter he subscribed to. There was no rhyme or reason to what he read.

He always said to me, *"At night, just before I close my eyes, I'm going to read something that has to do with marketing every single night of my life. Why? Because I want my mind concentrating on something positive, something I can think about while I sleep… so when I wake up, I hit the ground running."*

He recognized that his own book had to be a tangible, physical representation of his knowledge and expertise, and could help to establish his credibility and authority in his field of expertise as a consultant.

With this in mind, JIM set out to write a book that would showcase his expertise and serve as a valuable resource for potential clients.

Once his book was published, he sat on a Zoom with me, told me his story, and I went to work on his book. It was done in 72 hours because he trusted in me and my decisions.

Then once he had it, he began distributing it everywhere he went. Copy shops, restaurants, networking events, parties, and fast food joints.

He gave signed copies to friends, family, and colleagues, and even left them in waiting rooms and coffee shops. One time he went to the airport and left ten copies in the bookstore knowing full well someone would pick them up.

JIM's strategy paid off in a big way.

By giving away his book consistently, he was able to showcase his knowledge and expertise to his potential clients, who were impressed by his insights and recommendations inside his book.

As a result, JIM doubled his consulting business in less than ninety days. He was a doer, not a talker.

By using his book as his ultimate business card, JIM was able to establish himself as a trusted authority in his field and attract new business opportunities.

He recognized that the value of his book extended far beyond its cover, and that by sharing a tiny portion of his expertise with other people, he could build meaningful relationships and grow his business. JIM's success serves as a powerful example of the impact that one single book can have on one's business.

Your takeaway is this. By creating and distributing a good lead generation book that showcases your expertise, you can establish yourself as a thought leader and attract new business opportunities that can help to take your career to new heights.

Lead magnets like this can come in many different forms, including eBooks, whitepapers, webinars, checklists, and free trials, but a print book is the ultimate business card because it's REAL and people can 'touch' it as well as 'feel' it. It's very powerful.

The key most people forget is to offer something that is both enticing and relevant to your target audience, so that those people are "motivated" to exchange their contact information for your content. If you give them content, something of value, they'll want more.

So how can a lead magnet help you make more money? By capturing the contact information of potential customers, you can begin to build a long term relationship with them.

BTW, there are multiple opportunities, gifts and bonuses at the end of this short book, so make sure you take advantage of them. They're not your usual hype. They are what I call real bonuses where you can opt in and get some really good reports, downloads, consulting etc.

By providing people, who will be your readers, with the necessary follow up, you'll be staying in touch with them through multiple avenues including:

- email marketing campaigns,
- blog posts,
- print newsletters, and
- emotional direct mail,

… plus when you do this you can establish yourself as an authority and build the all important trust factor with your audience.

As you continue to 'nurture' your leads, which you have to do that at least three or four times a month, you provide them with opportunities to invest in your products or services with an ongoing touch campaign that is not salesy nor manipulative. This is where the rubber meets the road.

By targeting individuals who have already expressed interest in your content and have provided you with their contact information, you increase your chances of converting them into paying customers and client's.

This is your ultimate goal with your short lead generation book.

Overall, a lead magnet like this is an essential tool for any business, entrepreneur or professional looking to generate more leads when will then increase their revenue.

All I can tell you is this. It just works.

PERIOD.

If you can hand out business cards, imagine how strong it is to hand out a lead generation book so people can get to know, like and trust you.

Your books can and will be one of your legacies.

When you offer valuable content and building real relationships with your potential customers, patients and clients, you turn your leads into loyal clients who are eager to do business with you.

If that's what you want, and I believe it is, do me a favor. Keep reading. I've got more for you in the next chapter.

This book was written just for you.

CHAPTER 2
CHOOSE THE RIGHT
LEAD MAGNET.

MARY was an interesting client. She thought everything needed to be perfect if she was going to publish a book.

I got her over that belief as fast as I could. She persisted, but I won. Once her book was published, MARY began distributing it everywhere she went.

She was like JIM. She listened to what I

told her so she gave copies to all her friends, family, and colleagues. She even left them in waiting rooms and coffee shops because I told her what JIM did.

By passing out multiple copies of her book every month, with pig headed determination, MARY was able to showcase her knowledge and expertise to potential clients.

If someone didn't want her book, she smiled and moved to the next person. She was thoughtful and didn't just hand it to anyone.

She looked at someone and if they looked like they could become a client, she made conversation with them and bestowed upon them a signed copy of her brand new book.

As a result, MARY's book helped her to establish herself as a 'trusted' authority in her industry, and attract some really good, qualified new business opportunities.

She was able to build meaningful relationships with potential clients and generate leads that converted into paying customers which was her ultimate goal.

It's a simple system. Write a book with me. Get it on Amazon. Put a price tag on it, and then order multiple copies. It's that simple. Once it's on Amazon for say $25.00 you can tell people, "Would you mind if I gave you a $25.00 GIFT today?" Most are happy to receive a book.

Then she'd say, *"Do me a favor. Read it, it'll take you about 30 minutes, then give it to someone that needs help making more money. Pass it forward. Then tell the next person to read it and pass it on. My goal is to help as many people as I can with this book before the end of the year."*

She'd then smile, turn and walk away.

Today, MARY is able to stay home and work on her gardening hobby, while her book continues to work for her. She is still passing out more and more books.

She told me she'd never stop handing them out. Never! By creating a short, to-thepoint book with a specific call to action, MARY was able to provide value to her audience and generate new business opportunities for herself.

MARY's success serves as a powerful example of the impact that a book can have on one's business.

By using a book as an ultimate business card, entrepreneurs and authors can establish themselves as thought leaders in their industries and attract new business opportunities that can help to take their careers to new heights.

Choosing an ideal lead magnet is a critical step in any lead generation strategy.

Probably more important than realize. Let me share something else with you.

An effective lead magnet (something like this book) should be considered valuable, relevant, and compelling enough to motivate potential customers to exchange their contact information for your content.

That's the real ticket.

If you can generate people coming to your landing page, website, or connecting with you on Facebook or some other source, your book is the ultimate way to generate more leads.

Here are some tips for choosing your ideal lead magnet:

Know Your Audience: What's that mean? Let me put it to you like this. Start by identifying your target audience (new book coming out with 300 questions) and understanding their pain points, interests, and needs. This is mission critical to your success. Your lead magnet book should be "tailored" to your audience's specific needs and provide a solution to their problems. Be super clear on this and the rest is a walk in the park.

Solve a Problem: Your lead magnet (book) should offer a clear and practical solution to a problem that your target audience is facing. You can keep it simple or complicate it. This solution could be a guide, a checklist, a tutorial, or any other format that provides real value to your audience. I like short books with content because they give me the necessary space to write something that people can sink their teeth into. If they don't like you after you write your book, they'll probably never buy from you.

Offer Specific Benefits: Benefits are ten times better than features. If you don't know the difference, get my other books that talk about benefits and how to make those benefits help you stand out from all the noise. Make sure your lead magnet book clearly "communicates" the benefits of your product or service. Write the book, let it sit for 24-hours, then come back in a day or so and edit it. Make sure you ***highlight*** what makes your offer so unique and why your audience should choose you over your competitors.

DON'T MISS THIS POINT.

Keep it Simple: OMG… please keep it simple. If you bore someone, guess what happens? You guessed it. *You lose them.*

Your lead magnet should be easy to access, read, and consume.

That's why I suggest the short book. Whatever you do, avoid creating a lengthy or complicated piece of content that could "discourage" your potential customers from engaging with your offer. If they don't read it, nothing will most likely to happen.

Test and Optimize: Once you have created your lead magnet book, 'test it' with a small sample of your target audience to see how effective it is at generating leads. Use this feedback to 'optimize' your lead magnet book and start to improve its conversion rate. If you do this right, you shouldn't have to revise anything.

By following these simple tips, you can choose an ideal lead magnet book and title that resonates with your target audience and helps you to generate quality leads for your business, no matter what you do.

Remember, your book is your opportunity to showcase your expertise and build trust with your audience, so make sure you invest some time and resources into creating a high-quality offer that stands out from the competition. K.I.S. S. (Keep It Super Simple)

CHAPTER 3
THE MONEY IS IN THE LIST

People are confused. Most don't know what to do when they lose their job, or because of the economy, their business tanks. They forget what they offer the world and they forget about marketing themselves as an authority and expert.

In today's digital age, there are a plethora of marketing techniques and strategies available to businesses of all sizes.

One such strategy that has gained significant popularity in recent years is the use of lead generation books. I personally love books. That's why wrote this book in 3 hours for myself. It'll be on *Amazon* and if it sells, fine.

If not? No biggie. I can hand my lead generation books to lots of people.

If I pay $2.00 for a book, hand out 25 books a day and get a client that pays consulting fees of $500-$2,000/month is it a good investment for me? Yes, it is!!

These short books money making lead magnets are designed to provide valuable information to your potential customers in exchange for their "contact information", which can then be used for further marketing efforts from you with your follow up.

In this chapter, we will discuss the importance of writing a short lead generation book and why it is crucial to be persistent in handing it out.

You ready?

First and foremost, writing a short lead generation book is important because it can establish your business as an authority in your industry. You want to be the person that wrote the book on _____! You get that right?

By providing valuable information that your potential customers may not know, you are positioning yourself as an "expert" who can be trusted to provide high-quality products or services. This can lead to increased brand recognition, customer loyalty, and ultimately, sales.

WARNING: If you say you're going to do something, DELIVER. It's that simple. If you can't DELIVER, don't say you will.

Additionally, by offering a free resource, you are creating a positive experience for potential customers, which can lead to word-of-mouth referrals and positive reviews.

Another reason why writing a short lead generation book is important is that it can help you <u>build</u> your email list.

Email marketing is still one of the most effective ways to reach customers, with a potential return on investment of up to 4400%.

I tell my clients a few ways they can offer something in their book to get someone's email. With that email you can stay in contact with people for years as long as they don't delete your contact and opt out. If you're not boring, they will not opt out.

By offering a free resource in exchange for contact information, you are building a list of potential customers who have already shown interest in your business. They may say "NO" today, but what they are really saying is, "Not Yet."

This list can then be used to promote new products or services, offer exclusive discounts, or simply keep in touch with customers to maintain brand awareness.

Email marketers know their LIST is

something that can make them money. There was a woman that I share with my clients that had a small list.

She kept growing it and a few years later it was like 14,000 people. When she made an offer for a $2,500 service only 1% would buy but 1% of 14,000 is [140 times $2,500] = $350,000.

It's not a bad thing to have good people who trust you on your list. Make an offer every month, and grow your income.

In addition to building your email list, a short lead generation magnet book can also help you qualify your leads.

Not everyone who downloads, buys it on Amazon or gets in line to have it given to them will be a good fit for your business, but those who are -- can be "nurtured" into becoming "paying" customers.

By providing valuable information that is 'relevant' to your target audience, you are *attracting* the right people to your business.

This can save time and money in the long run, as you are not wasting resources on 'marketing' to people who are unlikely to convert.

Now that we've discussed why writing a short lead generation book is important, let's talk about why it's crucial and mission critical to be persistent in handing it out if you do nothing else.

You want your book to be the best and ultimate business card you've ever created. It can be if you're consistent and persistent.

The reality is that not everyone who visits your website or interacts with you will be ready to download your book right away if you work with me to get it in digital form.

This is important. Write this down.

In fact, it can take multiple touch points before someone decides to take action.

You have to be very persistent in handing out your book.

If you're sending it to people in a text or email you are increasing the likelihood that someone will eventually download it and potentially want it as a soft cover or hardcover book.

I can't say this enough.

Persistence can take many forms, from promoting your book on social media to offering it as a FREE bonus for attending a webinar or an event. If you're a speaker, you'll always want to hold your book up and talk about why you wrote it.

The key is to find "creative" ways to get your book in front of potential customers, without being pushy or salesy.

It's also important to track your results and adjust your strategy as needed. As my mentor Joel Bauer says, *"Test and watch the reactions of your audience. You always have to adjust to your audiences needs."*

If one approach isn't working, try something different until you find what works for your business at that particular event, party or webinar. Another reason why persistence is important is that it can help you stay "top of mind" with potential customers. It's so, so important.

Let's say you're doing a webinar. Even if someone isn't "ready" to download your book immediately, seeing your brand name or logo repeatedly can create familiarity and trust. The title is so-so important.

This can lead to increased engagement and eventually, a conversion. If you don't tell them why the book is important they will not want the download.

In conclusion, writing a short lead generation book can have many benefits for your business, from establishing yourself as an authority and expert to building your email list and qualifying your future leads.

However, it's important to be "persistent" in handing it out, as not everyone will be ready to take action right away. Again, some people have to THINK ABOUT IT, which is fine. They lose out. Not you.

By finding creative ways to promote your book and staying "top of mind" with potential customers and clients, you can increase your chances of success and ultimately, drive more sales for your business.

But make sure you have a CTA.

Crafting a compelling offer, also known as a *call to action* (CTA), is a critical component of any lead generation strategy.

A well-crafted CTA can motivate potential customers to take action and engage with your product or service.

I have a tendency to repeat myself when something is important, so if this sounds like something you've heard before, it probably is.

Repetition creates a new paradigm for you if you consistently repeat something.

Here are some tips for crafting a compelling offer that will resonate with your target audience:

Be Specific: Your CTA should be specific and clearly communicate the benefits of your product or service. Tell someone your call to action then ask them if they understand what you're offering.

You'll be surprised what they say if they are honest.

Avoid vague or general statements that don't provide a clear value proposition. You have to be super clear here, so spend the time and craft your message.

Provide a Hook: If you get nothing else out of this book, get this. A HOOK is everything. A hook is a *powerful statement or question* that captures your audience's attention and motivates them to learn more about your offer. Use a hook at the beginning, middle, and end of your book to keep your audience engaged and interested.

Here's an example: *"Would you like to generate an additional $5-10K every single month consistently like clockwork.... doing just one thing?"*

Make it Easy to Understand: Again, keep things simple. Your CTA should be easy to understand and actionable. I say once you've said it, someone should be able to repeat it back to you.

Try that out and find out if your CTA is simple. Use simple language and "avoid jargon or technical terms" that could confuse your audience. A confused audience will not buy. If you offer three or more options you're offering them too much and they will become confused and a confused mind does not BUY!!!

Offer Value: Your CTA should offer big massive value to your audience. This offer should be so good that they'd have to be crazy not to engage with you on your offer.

This amazing offer could be in the form of a free trial, a steep unannounced discount, a never before offered bonus, or any other incentive that motivates your audience to take action immediately.

Here's an example: *"If you call my office*

today, I'll give you 80% off your weight loss program and throw in a 90 Day 100% Money Back Guarantee if you don't lose at least 10 pounds following this program."

Use Urgency: Creating a sense of urgency can help to motivate potential customers to take action. Use time-limited offers or limited availability to create a sense of urgency and encourage your audience to act quickly.

Here's an example: *"Today is the last day to get your written for you BOOK at 50% OFF. That means at midnight, you'll pay the full fee versus say a $2,500 fee at the entry point. But remember. You have to text me at: (951) 760-0798 today or the deal is gone for good and I'm a man of my word."*

By following these simple tips, you can craft a compelling offer that resonates with your target audience and motivates them to engage with your product or service.

Remember, your CTA is your opportunity to showcase the value of your offer and build trust with your audience.

BONUS ONE

Keeping your book short is essential for a successful strategy. You'll want to study what I did in this book as well as how I made offers throughout it.

I've made this book a digital book as for obvious reasons.

There are several reasons why you want to keep your lead magnet book short, and they all revolve around the idea of providing good value to your potential customers while respecting their time.

Firstly, a short lead magnet like this book is more likely to be read if given to them personally or "downloaded!" **Here's why**!

In today's fast-paced world, where everyone is saying their prospects have a TikTok attention span, people have limited attention spans.

That means they want information that is easy to digest and quickly actionable.

By keeping your lead magnet book short, you are providing your prospects with the right amount of information without overwhelming them with too much to read.

Question: How many books can you write if you write 40-50 pages on one subject. A subject that you know?

This short book will increase the likelihood that they will download and read it, which ultimately can lead to you getting more leads and sales for your business.

Secondly, a short lead magnet book allows you to focus on providing high-quality, actionable content that can be read in less than one hour.

When you have a 'limited' amount of space to work with, you need to 'prioritize' the most important information and make it as clear and concise as possible.

This forces you to "cut out any fluff or filler content" and *focus* on providing value to your potential clients.

By doing so, you are more likely to establish yourself as an authority in your space plus build more trust with your audience.

Thirdly, a short book is easier and quicker to create. Creating a long book requires more time, resources, and effort and most people will not read a long book.

This is especially important if you are running a time-sensitive promotion or want to capitalize on a trending topic. One of my clients, Celia likes to create books for each event she goes to. That way people are ready to read the book because it's current.

Lastly, a short lead magnet book allows you to leave your potential customers wanting more. If you provide too much information in your lead magnet book, (which is a big no no), your potential customers may feel like they already have everything they need which means they won't be motivated to take further action.

By keeping your book short and focused, you can pique their interest and leave them wanting to learn more about your business and what you have to offer. That's what a lead generation book is all about.

This is crucial for a successful lead generation strategy.

If you provide value to your potential customers while respecting their time, you can increase the likelihood that they will download or take the time to read your book, which again will establish you as an authority, and build trust with your audience. Once someone trusts you, your chances of selling them something increase big time.

BONUS TWO

Let me ask you this. "Are you tired of struggling to generate leads for your business?"

"Do you want to become a recognized authority, expert and celebrity?"

Then it's time to take action and invest in a lead generation book.

At https://ivancarney.com , I specialize in helping you with your health, but at https://bookandmoney.com/call I can talk to you about creating high-quality lead generation books that are "tailored" to your business and audience.

SIDENOTE: If you're like one of my clients, and you think you know more than me, then by all means, don't work with me. Give me control, give me a simple outline and I'll create your book. Then you get two revisions. If that fits your criteria, then contact me.

My process is simple and efficient - you give me a one-hour interview on Zoom, and I'll take care of the rest.

Within (72) hours, if you are in a rush to get a book completed, you'll have a lead generation book similar to this one that's ready to be printed on *Amazon*, complete with a title and cover.

You just find someone to put it on *Amazon* or I have a contact that will do that for a minimal amount and you're off to the races.

My books have helped countless

businesses establish themselves as experts in their industry, generate leads, and increase sales.

One of my clients actually paid $40,000 to have his book written for his solar company. I thought it was a bit much, but hey, what can I say.

Here's the best part? My prices start at a minimum of $5,000 and go up from there, but you will get your money's worth for sure. This is a small investment when you consider the potential return on investment. If you are reading this paragraph, you can get a discount if you mention this page and this offer.

So, if you're ready to take your business to the next level and become a recognized authority, it's time to take action.

Book a free 15-minute consultation with me today by visiting the link below:

https://bookandmoney.com/call.

I'll answer any questions you may have

and provide you with more information on how our lead generation books can benefit your business.

Don't wait any longer to start generating leads and becoming a celebrity in your industry. Contact me today and let's get started!

I almost forgot. If you email me at doccarneymarketing@gmail.com and tell me that you invested in this book, I'll send you something you will not expect. Street value of that item: hundreds of dollars. I'm not kidding, but again, you'll have to show me proof that you actually invested in this book.

I'll also give you something that I've been working on for years, but I only want to share that with people that actually read this book.

FINAL THOUGHTS
FROM
DR. CARNEY

Why is it so important to write a book like this and establish instant credibility before you even open your mouth?

Can you imagine going to an event and you leave your ultimate business card (the short book) on everyone's chair. It's not a business card.

It's the ultimate business card that is short, sweet and to the point. If they want to connect with you they can. Books have real value and who would get mad at getting something for FREE that has some REAL VALUE?

Writing a lead generation book is crucial for establishing instant credibility in your industry. '

By creating a book that provides valuable information to your potential customers, you are positioning yourself as an authority and expert in your field.

This can help you stand out from your competition, attract more leads, and ultimately increase sales.

In addition, a lead generation book is the ultimate business card like I said. Don't forget that.

This is a huge takeaway.

Instead of handing out a traditional business card, you can leave your book on everyone's chair at an event, providing them with something that has real value.

People are more likely to hold onto a book than a business card, and they will remember the [value] that you provided them with.

This can lead to more connections, referrals, and ultimately, more business.

Another advantage of a lead generation book is that it can help you establish a relationship with your potential customers before you even open your mouth.

When someone reads your book, they are getting to know you and your business.

They are learning about your expertise and the value that you can provide to them.

This can help "build" trust and credibility, making it "easier" for you to convert them into paying customers.

In conclusion, writing a lead generation book is a powerful tool for establishing instant credibility in your industry, standing out from your competition, and attracting more leads.

By providing value to your potential customers through a short and sweet book, you can position yourself as an authority, build trust and credibility, and ultimately, increase sales.

So, if you want to take your business to the next level, it's time to invest in a lead generation book (my friend, Mike Capuzzi calls a SHOOK) and start reaping the benefits!

How to get ahold of me directly:
doccarneymarketing@gmail.com
or
https://bookandmoney.com/call
This is an important video that is 3 minutes long if you have the time.
https://www.loom.com/share/c3a0e84857 964ca088bf550efe5f8bc0

I thought I had the QR code thing down, but as you can see on page 41, I don't apparently.

But that doesn't matter.

I'll work on that for the next book.

Just know this one thing. I'm here to help you become a better marketer, a healthier person, and get CLEAR on what it is you can do better than most people so you can help your family and friends become exactly what they want to become.

This book was written just for you.

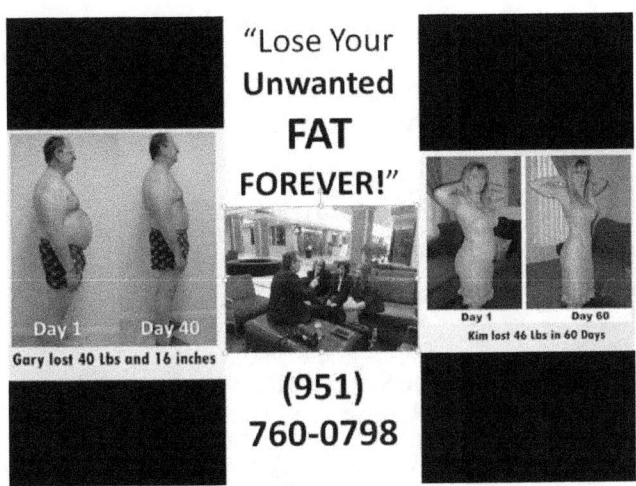

CHAPTER 7

THIS IS THE OOPS CHAPTER

If you decide to work with me to create your lead generation book, you will receive a **FREE** one-hour session with me privately on Zoom. If we happen to go over that one hour, there will be **NO CHARGE**. I'm here to help you and I want you to get your book written and published on *Amazon*.

This session is designed to help me to answer any questions you may have after your book is completed.

It's my way of ensuring that you have all the information and support you need to make the most of your book.

Creating this special lead generation book - can be an incredibly powerful tool for growing your business if you do it.

Once your book is done, you will have a valuable resource that you can use to attract new leads and establish yourself as an expert in your business or profession.

However, it's important to know how to utilize your book to its fullest potential.

During our one-hour session, I will answer any questions you have about how to promote your book by handing it to people, what to say, how to use it to generate leads, and how to maximize your return on investment.

We will discuss the strategies that have been successful for other businesses and tailor them to your specific needs and goals.

By working with me, you will not only

have a high-quality lead generation book, but you will also have the knowledge and expertise to make the most of it.

I want to ensure that you have everything you need to succeed, and that's why I offer this free one-hour implementation session.

Remember, if you craft your book properly and utilize it to its full potential, follow the protocol - it can generate thousands of dollars for your business.

It's not just about writing a book, it's about knowing how to promote it, how to use it to generate leads, how to follow up, what to say when you follow up and how to leverage your book to establish yourself as an expert and the only logical choice.

With my help, you will have all the tools and knowledge you need to make the most of your book and therefore, grow your business.

So, if you're ready to take your business to the next level, you can implement and invest in 500-1000 lead generation books after you have your system down; contact me as soon as you can. My team and I will help you get started and get you registered for your *free one-hour implementation session with me.*

That is a $2,000 value. If you do that as soon as you purchase this book, I'll give you 3 **FREE REPORTS** as well that will get you on your way to making more money!

I enjoyed writing this book, and I want you to know. I'll be writing a series of 50 NEW books in about 45 days.

They'll be for any profession. Plumbers, doctors, therapists, speakers, authors, workforce specialists, attorneys, holistic practitioners, stay at home moms, etc. If you want me to write one for your profession or business, reach out to me at: doccarneymarketing@gmail.com

Watch for the book. It'll be written by me and it'll be one of the best books you've ever read. This is the Oops Chapter. Hope it made sense to you, but it's been fun writing this short book.

I could have made this book longer. In fact, me just writing what I've written has given me 3 more ideas on 3 more short books. Again, you can do exactly what I'm doing if you just get out of your own way.

Listen, you know more about you than anyone else. You know what upsets you. You know what makes you smile.

You know what can make you cry and you know what will get your blood heated. Write your book, get it formatted, edited and get it out there.

If someone gives you some feedback that you don't like, you have two choices. Change it, or know that everyone has an opinion.

You can bow down and say, "Oh I wrote something bad," or you can say to yourself, "She has an opinion, and I respect it, but I'm still going to tell you my point of view and I'm sticking to it."

I said this was the OOPS Chapter for a reason. This is where I basically write anything I want to write without it meaning anything unless you take a deep dive with me and we figure it out together. I'm here for you. Just reach out.

This book was written just for you.

www.ingramcontent.com/pod-product-compliance
Lightning Source LLC
Chambersburg PA
CBHW070757220526
45467CB00014B/678